# Soft Parts of the Back

# University of Central Florida
# Contemporary Poetry Series

# Soft Parts of the Back

POEMS BY

## Daryl Ngee Chinn

UNIVERSITY OF CENTRAL FLORIDA PRESS

ORLANDO

Library of Congress Cataloging-in-Publication Data

Chinn, Daryl Ngee.
    Soft parts of the back: poems / by Daryl Ngee Chinn.
        p.   cm.—(University of Central Florida contemporary poetry
    series)
    ISBN 0–8130–0922–7 (cloth) (alk. paper)
    ISBN 0–8130–0938–3 (paper)
    I. Title. II. Series.
PS3553.H4898S64   1989
811'.54—dc19        89–4663
                        CIP

University Presses of Florida is the central agency for scholarly publishing of the
State of Florida's university system, producing books selected for publication by
the faculty editorial committees of Florida's nine public universities. Orders for
books published by all member presses should be addressed to University
Presses of Florida, 15 NW 15th Street, Gainesville, Florida 32603.

# Acknowledgments

Some of these poems have appeared in the following magazines and anthologies, whose editors I thank.

**The Florida Review** published "Allison Cries, Granma Died, Zero" under the title, "You're so Vain or They're so Smart"; and "My Knees, My Hips, My Fist" originally appeared as "Look Both Ways."

"I stand naked and flatfooted" first appeared in **Pendulum**.

**The Greenfield Review** published "Not Translation, Not Poetry."

**Toyon** published "Libraries," "Pruning," "Words, like Rice and Snow," "Diener Cooks," and "Silences."

**The Florida Review** published "Hanging in the Shop," "A Small Part in *Annie Get Your Gun*," and "Three."

# Contents

*Soft Parts of the Back*

# Allison Cries, Granma Died, Zero

Baltimore, a summer swamp night
and my week-old daughter and I rock
slowly. She is as long
as one arm. I use two
to keep her limp neck straight.

My grandmother, in California,
has just died.
> How is the baby's mother
> Phyllis doing? is all
> Mom said she said. I'll miss her
> funeral.

How am I supposed to keep
the baby's head from falling?
In the crook of my elbow. She stirs.

First, I remember
that I do not remember. I know
> my wife does not speak Chinese,
> and I do not know enough
> to start easily.
So do what, I'm asking. This daughter
is here,
is, here, now. How shall she be?
What shall she be? What
am I?

In Switzerland,
we went to a Chinese restaurant,
and in Chinese, I asked for a cheap meal. Suddenly,
fed up with my stuttering, the man yelled,

"Will you please speak English?" The accent
could have been Indiana, Iowa, Nevada,
Hicksville, Omaha, Seattle.

Tender, love, cuddle, embrace, kiss, caress:
in French, I can say these.
I know them in English, but
we seldom did these at home, my parents'
Chinese suburban home where we got good grades,
"Get good grades, *dead you.*" Yet
the first thing I asked my father was,
Will you give her a Chinese name?
In weeks, years, and visits to come,

How did we coo? What was embrace?
Was there love? Did we caress? Show us.

The hugs came from my grandmother.
The language, then, also comes from her.

How, then, do I start?

From the beginning, of course:
*Aiee ya,* but you are beautiful, though small.
Don't cry. Is your diaper wet? Go
to sleep.

The words sound
foreign.

# *Lying in a Dream*

The beginning must have been like this:

He started
when he could stand this nothing
no longer, after
he had been
in an empty, colorless sky,
heatless, not able to shiver
or sit down or get up, full
of all possibilities, without
the daring of one failure.

Dark undressing
the dark, slant light
aiming for the eyes.

There was only one
indescribable fact,
and it had no drama or audience. Everything
was one big word, bigger
than all entropy, nothing
under everything.

The barest of heartbeats.

Zero,
infinity.

# Words, like Rice and Snow

"My rice always comes out too mushy," said Laurie.
Use less water, I told her. "But the recipe says
two cups of water for each cup of rice." Forget
the recipe, I said. Just enough water
to cover your knuckles.

In a Chinese restaurant, once, my brother ordered
for my sister, me, and him. "Three bowls
of uncooked rice," he said in Chinese
to the waiter, who hesitated
and brought us steaming cooked rice.

In college anthropology, Dr. Dietz
mentioned to us eight hundred students that Eskimos
use twenty-two names for snow. He didn't tell us
what any of those words were.

Across the bay from San Francisco, in El Cerrito,
there wasn't much snow where Granma was living
with Mom and Dad. Nor was there much
in the Pearl River delta near Canton, China, where Dad
and Granma grew up. So I asked them about the Chinese
words for rice.

Granma said she was too tired to remember.
Soon she was going to sleep anyway,
so why bother? I waited
until she started to eat lunch with Dad,
and then I asked again. At first,
they were quiet. It was forty years
since either had been back. Then

Dad spread his hands to show how tall
shoots and plants and stalks grew
before they changed names or had to be thinned
or cut. Only poor people ate brown rice, he said.

Granma forgot her lunch, got up, hit her head
on the hanging lamp, moved back and forth,
bent again and again over the floor,
pulled up and put down
shoots on Mom's patterned linoleum.
She said you had to stoop all day
in a field flooded ankle deep
and take each shoot from down in the mud
and put it somewhere else in the mud, *aiee ya*,
growing rice was such hard and tiring work.

Uncooked rice, cooked rice, rice crust, rice porridge,
rice crust broth, rice flour, rice noodles—

I asked my father how to say hello
in Chinese. All he knew
was the English word with his shy lilt
and, "Have you eaten any rice?"


Yesterday we had guests at dinner,
snow fungus soup, steamed chicken,
bean threads and Chinese sausage,
broccoli and black mushrooms in oyster sauce,
rice. My wife had gone to pick up our daughter
from rehearsal, and everyone was eating fast
so we could go to a movie. When Annette,
the babysitter, came early, I opened the door.
"Have you eaten yet?" I asked.

# Trying to Find My Father

When I try to remember my father and his family,
it is my mother or her mother I see
washing vegetables in the kitchen,
or my grandmother's apron that smells of oil,
onions, garlic, soap,
like a handful of wet bamboo chopsticks
just before I roll them up in a dish towel.
*********

I can only see the back of my father's head
as we ride to San Francisco on Sunday
to visit his brother. When we arrive,
my mother says, "Say hello
to Uncle and Aunt Six." Then
we go to find our cousins' comic books.
Maybe we also go to visit Uncle Sam,
who is Uncle Two, at his grocery store
with the dark wood floor,
but my father doesn't say much,
and I still see just the back of his head.
Perhaps he has a hat on.
*********

Questions have become the darknesses.
They're not as simple as asking my father
to take us to Chinese school or to close the laundry
before nine every night or all day Sunday.
Once I start, there will be more questions.
The darkness enlarges.
*********

He tells us he lived in New York City
and Utah. He used to drive through Idaho,
Nevada, Wyoming, Arizona, and New Mexico
to find Chinese who would buy China Bonds.
At one time, my mother says,
he could walk into any Chinese restaurant
in those states and get a free meal

because he had trained the cooks
in his brother's Salt Lake City restaurant.
　　　　\*\*\*\*\*\*\*\*

A snapshot of him leaning against a post
at sixteen in Temple Square in Salt Lake:
he's wearing knickers, and he's smiling.
　　　　\*\*\*\*\*\*\*\*

Why join any church, he's always said.
Just take the best from them all.
　　　　\*\*\*\*\*\*\*\*

In the first grade, my friends asked me
how old my parents were. "Tell them I'm ninety-eight,"
said my dad. Mrs. Dollar, my teacher,
called to make sure.
　　　　\*\*\*\*\*\*\*\*

My mom was the one who swung her chopsticks
at us at the dinner table
or washed our mouths out with soap.
One time I told her to shut up. My father
slapped me, the only time he ever did that.
　　　　\*\*\*\*\*\*\*\*

When I was leaving for college, I told him
I didn't know if there would be any Chinese
grocery stores or restaurants in Baltimore.
Just do the best with what you have, he said.
　　　　\*\*\*\*\*\*\*\*

He sent his four children and wife to college,
built a house in the El Cerrito hills,
reads Chinese and English books
at the kitchen table, in the bathroom,
on the couch.
　　　　\*\*\*\*\*\*\*\*

When I was trying to remember my Chinese,
I asked him why we never lived in Chinatown.
He could have said, We escaped tuberculosis.
There are a lot of lonely old men there. You
had a place to roller skate and ride bikes,
a lawn to roll on, a piano at home,

a library nearby.
Instead, he just told me,
Things weren't so good in Chinatown.

*********

My mother says that last year
one of my father's family from the village
was talking about us children.
"Isn't one of your sons married to a foreigner?"
the woman asked.
"Yes," said my dad, "but she's given me
two beautiful grandchildren."

*********

Last night I got angry at my daughter
for not practicing, slapped and shook her
for not obeying my wife. Some other time
I might have just yelled. I didn't understand my anger.
What I saw was that it was getting late,
that soon she was going to have no time
to do homework before dinner. And after dinner,
it would be time for bed. It was going to be dark.

# Not Translation, Not Poetry

—for those who felt "cheated"
at reading "The Laws" in China Men

Ask the old men in Chinatown,
the ones who washed and ironed in laundries,
cooked in restaurants, fished in San Francisco Bay,
laid rocks and track from California to Utah
and then down to Los Angeles.
These old men remember
that the rocks and snow in the Sierras
are softer and warmer than memories
of interrogators and officials on Angel Island
who said, "It is my duty to question your past,
to find out if you know where the stove was
back in your home in China. And it is my judgment
that this man who calls himself your brother
and these women who claim to be your wife and mother
are liars and will be sent back to China."

These men never had a wife to rub their tired shoulders
or to warm their bed. They never had children
climbing their laps or searching their pockets
for quarters or candy.
They never heard their mothers complaining
or saw them washing vegetables.
Even if they had owned all the tea in China,
they never drank tea with their brothers again.

That short chapter
in the middle of a book
about Chinese-American dreams fulfilled
has no darkness for your dreaming,
no scenery, demons, romance, epic,
only a spotlight on
laws, numbers, facts, dates,
history you and I
should have learned in the eleventh grade.

Go back and ask your teachers
about the California Congressman who used eloquence
and power in 1882 to argue and lobby for
the exclusion, from the pursuit of happiness in America,
of all Chinese laborers
        —would-be laundrymen, houseboys,
            fishermen, farmers, cigarmakers, gravediggers—
and about the Congressman who wrote the law
that kept all Chinese women
from entering the United States
from 1902 to 1946. Wasn't that when
your grandparents came to America?

Ask the white women who never asked their husbands
why they killed Chinese
in Utah, after they finished the railroad in 1865,
in Los Angeles in 1871,
in Rock Springs, Wyoming, in 1885.
Ask the kids who ran to the docks in 1886
to watch their fathers put pigtailed men
on steamboats in Humboldt Bay.

Ask Judge Kaufman of Detroit
who said in 1982
that Robert Ebens and Michael Nitz,
who killed Vincent Chin with a Louisville Slugger,
could have probation and a suspended fine
because Vincent Chin looked Japanese.

Pretend you are Caucasian and pregnant
like Christina Tien of Grand Ledge, Michigan.
It is New Year's Day, 1985.
Imagine how much warmth and softness
you feel when four men with knives
slash your car tires outside in the snow,
break your living room windows with crowbars
and say, "We want to speak with your husband
and any other Chinks in the house."

You don't understand my anger
and I am embarrassed, yet we can sit
here among the linen and silver
in this candlelit restaurant and talk
about the red snapper, the spinach fettucine
with dill and too much garlic, just
the way I like it.

If you still don't understand,
let's say that you and I
got illegally married in Maryland
—you're white, I'm not—
and let's imagine that it is Ching Ming,
that we are pulling weeds from and putting out tea
on Grandfather's grave in China.
Talk. Ask Grandfather's grave spirit to tell you
more than he told my father,
who came to America to be with his brothers.
Ask Grandfather why the only thing he said
about his stay in America was, "Don't send your sons
to Gold Mountain."

# Libraries

When I was nine, some
schoolmates and their parents, white people
in Richmond, California,
greeted us politely
when we met at the shoes in Penney's.
But after school one day
I pulled Ronald Koski into a dry ditch
after he called me a Chink
and a real estate man wouldn't show us
houses near the library.

One night at dinner
in our Wall Avenue house
Mom said that
when we came home from Pullman School
we three kids were going to Chinese school.
Years later, I would find out
that only Orthodox or Chassidic Jewish children
do something like this:

at 3:30 for six straight years
Mom got us into the Packard or Plymouth
and drove us twenty miles to Oakland
to the Chinese Community Center.

Days I sat next to Gailyn Sparks,
practiced my capital Ds,
learned how to multiply,
and listened to Lars Solander
imitate the whine and scream
of Stukas and Messerschmitts;
evenings I memorized Chinese characters
with Barbara Gong and Raymond Eng
and played warball
with Benjamin Kwon and Jones Lee.
In time, I easily held a brushpen

and learned to give proper shape and place
to every stroke, started essays about Han emperors
down from top right.

Mom always stayed in Oakland
those two hours of school,
sometimes just in the car
with our empty dinner bowls and spelling books.
We never checked on her, even during recess.
The second winter she carried my newborn sister
to the Chinese markets before they closed
and then drove over to the Oakland library.

Today, twenty years later,
I have a daughter, Allison,
and we live in Maryland,
across the country from Richmond and Oakland.
During the day I tie her small shoes
and take her for walks
to the new library here in Towson.
Some evenings I phone my mother.
I tell her I don't know
some Chinese words I want to teach my daughter,
words like turtle, dragon, taxicab.
"Give me a second," she says.
I wait, listening to the hiss,
while she remembers.

# Skin Color from the Sun

I used to be
an admissions counselor
at Humboldt State University.

One day Penny, our secretary, told me to
pick up Line One.
I talked to this man from Palo Alto
about life in the dorms,
          the low cost of movies and rent,
          whether his daughter would need a car,
          the friendly people,
          the small classes of ten or fifteen.

When we were done, he thanked me
and asked my name. Daryl Chinn, I said.
Oh, he said, you speak very good English.
Where are you from?
I grew up in Richmond and El Cerrito, California, just
across the bay and north of where you're
calling from, I said.
Well, he said, where were you born?
Salt Lake City, I said.
Well then, where were your parents from?
My mother's from Austin, Texas, but
her brothers and sisters were born
in Washington, D.C., and Utah and—
—no, he interrupted, where
were your ancestors from?
Using the California English I had learned
from my mother and father,
from my teachers at Pullman Elementary,
Granada Junior High, and Harry Ells High,
I said, My father is from Southern China,
my voice flat and dead.

I wanted to ask him,
Where did you learn to speak English so well?
Where are you from, really
from?

       \*\*\*\*\*\*\*\*

My wife and I spent a year in Florida teaching
at the University of Central Florida in Orlando.
One day, we were waiting at a stop light
near our kids' grade school. A busload
of junior high students pulled alongside.
Someone yelled out the window,
Go home Vietnamese.

       \*\*\*\*\*\*\*\*

Sticks and stones will break my bones
but names can never hurt me.

Bullshit.

       \*\*\*\*\*\*\*\*

I, a Chink, married this Yid broad.
Our kids are half-breeds, mulattos.
We drive Frog and Nazi cars,
play a Jap stereo with gook speakers
and flatlander turntable.

       \*\*\*\*\*\*\*\*

In the high school locker room
one day just after we showered,
Lon, next to me,
said white boys smelled funny.
When I looked at him, he held his nose
and pointed silently at Jay
behind us. Later, at lunch time,
Jay said that without nigger boys
Coach wouldn't have a basketball team.

That year, just before I went to college,
Aunt Annie said, "Just remember,
since you're Chinese, they

can't tell what you are. Black people
won't think you're white. White people
won't know if you're colored.
Both might trust you. You can be
on either side. Use your race
to be whatever you want to be."
                \*\*\*\*\*\*\*\*\*
Chinese are
        —inscrutable, mysterious, unsmiling
        —mathematical
        —docile, unassertive, quiet
        —all skinny, all short
        —meticulous, precise
        —all martial artists
        —hairless, odorless
        —good ping pong players
        —poor English speakers
        —studious
        —nearsighted
        —devious
        —obsequious, sycophantic
        —ancestor worshippers
        —good cooks and laundry workers
        —all engineers, doctors, or optometrists
        —a model minority
        —not poets
        —other_____
                \*\*\*\*\*\*\*\*\*
For a very long time in Europe,
Jews were forced into ghettos,
where their lives were circumscribed—
where they could live, what they could be,
who their friends could be,
where they could travel.
Some Jews found their ways out of the ghetto.
They intermarried, changed their names,
converted to Christianity,
became doctors, lawyers, royal advisors,

university scholars, and moved into
non-Jewish neighborhoods.

During the Holocaust, Adolf Hitler
convinced blond, blue-eyed women
to have babies fathered by
blond, blue-eyed men.

During the Holocaust,
if a man or woman or child
had even one grandparent who was Jewish
that person went to the ovens.

Even the children of those
blond, blue-eyed parents,
if their skin or hair or eyes
turned dark,
went to the ovens.
                *********

My children come home
with questions, complaints, reports.
My son asks, Are we half-Jewish, half-Chinese?
My daughter complains, Someone
called me a China doll.

How can we tell
what part of you is Jewish or Chinese?
I ask them. Your right eye? Your left shoulder?
Your bones? The skin below your belly button?
Tell them your ancestors came from China,
that your mother is Jewish. Tell them
you are all, both.
                *********

Let's go to my house,
eat some rice, some food,
talk about these words.
                *********

# Learning the Facts of Life

I am eight, and it is night.
My brother, sister, and I have been asleep for hours.
My mother opens the door, says, Go pee.
One by one we stumble into the bathroom,
sit, pee, and clump back into bed.
Mother pulls the blanket over my shoulders.
Heat from the hallway floods my face.
The lights go out. The heater clicks
and clicks, slower and slower.

From down the hall, noises.
Not talk, not sickness, not anger.
I'm falling back, back to sleep,
oh, yes, umm, oh ah yes

# Two Songs and a Three-Year-Old

What's a tune? she asked.

Why is it important?

I sang the words

    of "Baa Baa Black Sheep"

to the tune

    of "Home on the Range."

That's not right,

she said, knowing what is.

Baa, Baa, all day.

# A *Small Part in* Annie Get Your Gun

Leaning close to our bathroom mirror
our daughter puts on make-up:
base, eyeliner, eye shadow, mascara,
lipstick, blush.
At the hallway mirror
she twists left and right,
tilts her head from side to side,
watches the effect, practices
pose after pose.

Later, when she comes out on stage
with two shy girls, she giggles,
but her cheeks are flushed,
her eyelashes flutter,
she swings her hips,
sidles up to the man,
tilts her head.

Rejected, she looks hurt, touches her breast,
saunters away, fans herself, looks back
with a sidelong glance,
just a smirk, before slithering back to him.

In the empty auditorium
my wife and I gasp and moan.
All the times we've kissed, embraced,
and touched each other in the kitchen
in front of the children

and now this slender girl, thirteen,
flaunts her clear skin,

her waist-length hair, her large brown eyes, everything
for a tall baritone, a bad, bad, man.

I touch my wife's knee, we hold hands,
reassure ourselves this is only
a dress rehearsal.

# *Pruning*

When Wesley first started the violin
at seven, very little was easy or right.
How the fiddle stood it, I don't know.
His bow scratched across the strings,
which shrieked or whined. Often
I yelled, groaned and reached
for him. Draw the bow straight across
the strings, I said. Keep your chin tight.
That note is flat. Now it's sharp.
How do your know? he stomped. I know,
I screamed. Don't you believe me?
His tears dripped onto the brown violin.

Each winter
I take knives, saws, and clippers
to prune what
the year's longest nights have left.
Without leaves, the wind comes straight through
the wild branches of the Big Leaf Maple.
The roses and fuchsias
are frozen like dried snakes
piled up gray and brown.

Each winter
the sun aims at my eyes.
If I turn one way
there is more light,
but the branches darken.
If I move the other way,
my shadow falls through the branches.
Since light shows all
but tells nothing,
I have to say,
the trees and flowers
have only gone to sleep
or grown too wild,

so take a chance. Cut.
Come spring, the apple
will have good lavender flowers
and if you make stumps
of this fuchsia's overgrown madness,
in summer you'll have purple and crimson
lanterns in profusion.

This winter
I climbed out Wesley's window
and slung bunches of wet leaves
out of the rain gutters.
Suddenly, Wesley had climbed out
with his violin.
His fingers came down hard
on the ebony keyboard, and his hand drew the bow
straight across the strings.
He stood as sure
as a fiddler on the roof
while I had to lean toward him
to keep from falling.

# Regret for What Never

1. When the next song starts
   I'll get up and ask her to dance.

2. I owed him a letter.

3. It's just a small noise
   I'll fix later.

4. It just needs a coat of paint.

5. This won't take long.

6. Let's have lunch sometime.

7. One of these days
   I'll hug my father.

8. I didn't know how to
   let my son find out for himself.

9. I cooked it too long.

10. I cut too much off.

11. I can't afford to call her.

12. I should have let
    the knife fall.

13. I knew it was going to happen.

14. I'll write this down
    later.

# Hanging in the Shop

For her thirteenth Halloween
my daughter told me
she wanted to be
Death. She said
the ashen gray skull of her face
from which her brown eyes shone,
her black cloak,
and her hands painted like bones
were not enough. Would I make her
a scythe?

My mother's voice inside me wanted to say,
Don't try such things, they might come true now,
or, some other year,
or, no I won't, it's bad luck.
Then I remembered a long plank of ash
in my shop. I went out and ripsawed it
into seven long thin strips,
bent them all
into an S-curve that followed her
elegant sketch, glued and clamped them overnight.
The next day I spokeshaved
the curved handle smooth
and added a wooden blade painted silver.

When I gave it to her, I said
it was too beautiful for her to keep.
After Halloween, I unscrewed the blade
and hung the handle in the shop.
Now, suspended from thin fishing line,
it hovers over me whenever I work
out there.

## open field
## marsh and low tide

I am here to find the hawk

Gulls squat
and whine on the mud
Ducks float on the pond
a long flock of godwits
sparkles
and undulates
like a snake in the air
slithering
I stand still in the grass
and watch small cows in the far pasture
hear low rumbling trucks
hum

Across the field
close to the ground
leaning or swinging
right and left
back and forth
comes the marsh hawk

a thin shadow that flies so low
I can see her dark brown back
the white stripe
where the tail begins
She stops
turns
and drops
in her somersault
I can see her light belly
the dark and light wingstripes
outstretched talons
before she disappears

into the grass
then flaps her wings
three or four times
and flies off
with nothing

She lands
perhaps to rest
I edge closer
try to be quiet
but on dry grass my shoes
step on broken glass
she leaps straight up
all vees and double u's

This time she pumps and pumps
her wings and climbs higher
to the circling gulls
I can hardly see her
I wait and wait
while she soars
and soars

Just when I turn to leave
she glides by
close enough to talk to
I catch my breath
watch
her head turn
her stare and wink
then she is gone again
a thin shadow that moves fast
close to the ground

# Diener in the Kitchen

I rub ginger, garlic, and soy sauce
on a three and a half pound chicken
and roast it in a 325-degree oven for an hour.
As it cools, I ask the kids to set the table
and hone the big Chinese knife
back and forth, back and forth, on the steel.
Then, holding the left drumstick,
I chop down the back in one stroke
and again down the middle of the breastbone.
I splay the thigh joints and slice,
bend the wing joints and slice,
and thump, thump, chop the breast
away from the ribs and back. Thump.

It's like the morgue of Brookside Hospital
where I worked twenty years ago. Dr. Rolle,
the pathologist, already knows
why this black woman on the steel table died.
"Multiple myeloma," he says. "Watch."
He strokes his knives on the steel,
cuts the usual Y from her dark shoulders
down through the belly. Nothing is neat
inside, blood we suction flooded by more blood,
dripping onto the table, splashing on the floor.
The stomach, spleen, intestines, and liver
slip and ooze in our curious rubber hands
like my cool hands on my wife's
silk panties, the color unimportant.

"Look carefully at the bones," the doctor says.
He snaps a rib like a dry stick
and pokes the scalpel into her back.
The knife goes in as if her bones were skin.
"Just before she died," he says,
"something broke inside her
every time they turned her over."

My big knife chops the chicken
breast, thump, thighs, thump,
wings, and back, thump thump,
into bite-sized pieces
while juice flies and splatters.
If it's cooked just right,
each bone is bright red or pink inside,
blood and juice flow easily.
We eat the liver first before it gets cold.
The children keep the dark crispy skin for last.
I am the one who savors
the soft parts of the back.

# My Knees, My Hips, My Fist

Dad, writes my Mom,
has arthritis in his hips and legs.
He can't bend or move as fast
as he used to. But you know how it is
with him and doctors. Practically dies
before he goes and then
he's happy to get a clean bill.
Hope all is well. Best from us.

My father-in-law used to
eat ice cream every night. In Buffalo, once,
he ate three giant sundaes just because
someone made a bet he couldn't. Now,
he squirts his pee on a tab every month,
and his cuts heal slowly. We drive for him
at night, and his feet don't have much
flesh, so he doesn't dance. Yet
he makes us laugh about it all.

Granma said, when I was ten,
I don't know why my body hurts,
but pound my shoulders, my knees,
my thighs. Aah, good.
She started aching
that Salt Lake summer I was ten.
My fists were cheap medicine,
even though the family had to admit
that insulin was easier.
At ten, too, I was Superman.
Clean, hemmed rice-bag cape.
My glasses, however, didn't stay
in the phone booth,
but guided my swoops
through soft dry wheatgrass. Later,
they led hands and knees

on eight and a half foot jumps,
two to cross the living room.

I was born the day Congress stopped
saving time for World War Two.
I'm beginning to see.
Nineteen years ago, I was nineteen.

"*Ngee doy,*" Granpa said,
"I'm not being rude to your bride.
I'm just an old man waiting to die."
He was asking my twenty-four
to excuse his seventy.
It was still a strong voice
from a man who had always been
the size of a heartbeat.
Mom says he was afraid of fists
and insulin, so he stopped pounding Granma
after we started.

Allison, my daughter, is ten. She
jumps as far as she is tall. Yesterday,
when my son and I rode our bikes
around the neighborhood, he
wanted to race. Last week,
my hip ached and ached.

I hit it.

# Diener Cooks

I was twenty, still pre-med.
The morgue was like a fancy kitchen:
stainless steel sink, a big cutting board,
slicing, paring, boning knives, cleaver,
steel bowls, pots and pans hanging from
a rack on the ceiling,
even a scale and a meat saw,
lots of counter space.

In the middle of the cool room
was a long steel table with a drain
at one end. A body lay under a sheet.
Dr. Demay honed his knives,
uncovered an old Chinese man.
"Grampa," I started to yell,
"what are you doing here so soon?"

There wasn't time.
With a scalpel the pathologist
cut the usual Y
from the shoulders to the belly button.
Blood flowed, intestines,
liver, and spleen glistened,
smelled like stale garbage.
He cut and lifted them out one by one,
ran his rubbery hands over them,
used butcher knives to slice into them, looking for
why this man died, abscesses, tumors, something.
He reached between the bloody hips,
punctured and emptied the bladder,
cut out the kidneys and huge prostate.
Anything. Everything. Nothing.

With a special saw,
a round blade attached to a small stainless steel motor,
like a one-handed Green Machine,

he cut into the rib cage
the bones smelling like burning fat,
pried off the breastbone,
lifted the heart out, sliced and looked
at the arteries and veins.

We sawed open the skull:
I turned the head right or left
as he made a neat line from front to back.
He took the skullcap off carefully,
severed all the nerves,
lifted out the brain and sliced it
as my mother did when she cooked calf brain soup.
"Everything's normal," the doctor said.
Everything. Nothing.

I had to sit down.
Which one was my grandfather, this one or
the one who was
cooking at his restaurant in Salt Lake City?

At dinnertime these days in the kitchen
I yell for help. While the fan roars
and I am stir-frying broccoli,
tasting soup, sautéeing mushrooms,
and chopping the chicken,
I don't want to be alone, I don't want
it to be cold or quiet,
and even if there's nothing else to do,
I want my children
to watch me slice and stir, mix juice
or just wash stainless steel mixing bowls.
Set the table, get serving dishes, don't go away,
it's time to eat,
as I turn from the sink to the cutting board, to the stove,
and rush to put the whole meal
out at the same time.

# I stand naked and flatfooted

the shower water
jetstreams
points and trickles
falls
flows

steady   steady   glass spaghetti

small roar strange
no echo
attempts to press beyond
the skin

but
the glass and tile
could make
a hard   oversize
coffin

and shut

it off
hold tight

steady   steady

my skin looks smooth
I'm getting cold

# September. October. November.

Ever since we last saw each other
death has been a glow around my hands,
touched my letters,
stood next to me,
slept with me,
told me what to read and see.

The night I turned forty
I dreamt I photographed myself,
my face half dark, gone,
the shoulders bare, the face serious.
A woman was in the background
looking toward the camera.

The hanging fuchsia blooms
purple and crimson in the front yard.
Out back, the birch leaves glow
yellow in the long afternoons
even as the branches snake
darkly in the shadows.

On Halloween there was a letter
from Mrs. John Beall, Senior,
who said my friend and her son
John died in his sleep last week.
These last eight years I visited him
more than my brother.
The plans we made are frozen.
The letter he wrote
last month I can never answer.
What will his mother taste this autumn
each time she holds a teacup
and faces the slanting yellow light
on his ashes in her quiet garden?

When I was nine, my parents took me
to a birthday party for a seventy-year-old man.
He wore the Chinese happy color black,
and we gave him
red envelopes filled with money
for good luck and long life,
just as we do when friends or relatives
get married or have babies.

Last week, a bar bouncer
demanded proof of my age.
Big and dressed in dark clothes,
he growled, "Come here.
Where do you think you're going?"
A few days later, a man stopped me
during intermission at a concert.
He asked about the woman I played piano for.
"Is she your sister?"
I thought about how I had held the young woman
the day she was born, how I used to
take her back to her crib late at night,
how I had taught her what a tune was.
"She's my daughter," I said. "She's twelve."

John, I want you to come back.
Even though we would both be working,
there would still be time
for bicycling, dinners together,
concerts, talking. It would be
almost like beginning again.
I wouldn't mind so much
looking young as I get older, and I would feel lighter
in this dark dreaming if I could see you
walking in my garden as the branches break
open with light green leaves and pink blossoms
on mornings when my daughter is off with friends
playing her own music, before the mail arrives.

# The End of Imagination

Florida, the recreation area.
Sunny, flat.
A warm place where my wife and I can play
golf and tennis year round.

Thunderstorms, heat, humidity, and hurricanes
between April and November. Bugs that bite.
Where we will retire and live forever.
                    *********
I read the news and headlines
from the *Orlando Sentinel.*
I see this man's name
and imagine my own wife, my own life:
                    *********
The nurses said
Jess McNaughton visited his wife Lucille
every day, helping her with her cane, then the walker,
the wheelchair. They didn't know about
how he had yelled and screamed
at the bookkeeper, the insurance man,
the real estate man,
how he had sniveled to the bank loan officer,
gave up each dollar,
signed forms, called the kids
to tell them about each illness or fall,
scratched at the safe deposit box
for stock certificates,
the hundred shares of Eastman Kodak,
the twenty-year accumulation of Niagara Mohawk
and General Foods, her emerald ring,
his gold chain, her aquamarine necklace
to pay for his pneumonia, her broken hip,
her cataract surgery, and the deductible
on their trailer home found blown
across the field during the tropical storm
three years ago, and now

there was no money left,
how he couldn't read the street signs anymore,
how he spilled coffee
every time he poured or lifted a cup,
and how she had forgotten everything
except their wedding day fifty-three years ago
in Teaneck, New Jersey.
                    *********
It is New Year's Eve, three weeks
before Super Bowl in Miami,
when he puts the new pistol
under the seat of the white Dodge Dart
and goes to the nursing home.
He has thought about this day before,
practiced his motions while gazing at the lake
as the weather cooled and the humidity
went away, how he says hello
with the tip of his hat to Mrs. Carter,
the head nurse, signs his Lucille out
after helping her dress,
pushes the wheelchair out to the car,
lifts her light body into the front seat,
gently squeezes her bony thigh,
rearranges her gray hair,
pecks her lightly on the cheek
and closes the door gently.

He drives slowly out Highway 50,
past the shopping malls and condos under construction,
past dying cypress groves
and piles of burning orange trees,
heading west and south
toward the Bok Carillion Tower, the highest point
in southern Florida. Cars pass him, tourists
angry at this Sunday driver, an old man
who should be in a nursing home instead
of blocking their way to Disneyworld, EPCOT,
Circus World, Busch Gardens, Six Flags
Hall of Fame, Sea World, Cypress Gardens.
Old man, says one tourist father,

we have only two weeks before we go back
to New Jersey and winter.

He parks the car among the trees,
their oranges glowing in the dark green leaves.
"Aunt Bess and Uncle Joe called to say
they can't come tonight," says Lucille.
"They can't get out of Philly
because of the snow."
He thinks of their daughters in California
and Boston, their grandchildren, twelve, nine,
five. How will they get the news?
Who will tell them?

"Jessie, are we ready to start? Why
is it so quiet? Where is everyone?" She looks out
at the dirt, the trees, the sky,
and she smiles as she always has
when she is unsure of anything.
"In a moment, hon. Let me take off your glasses
and look into your eyes." He is gentle,
he kisses her, and he looks into her gray eyes,
the green flecks sparkling as they always have,
and he tries not to think as he cocks the gun,
holds it close to her ear
and pulls the trigger.
            *********
It is so much quieter now.
He opens the window and hears
a mockingbird rambling on, accusing,
taunting. Bitter. Cheap. Sleep. Sweet.
He closes the window,
looks at his silent wife, touches her cheek,
her shoulder, her hand. He remembers their wedding
night when it snowed and was silent outside,
the kids at their first baseball game
not knowing who to cheer for,
his fortieth birthday, a big party on the patio,
the feel of his granddaughter's hand
as they walked to the swimming pool last August,

the red dry cleaning tags for Tuesday,
the last time they lay together in the dark,
the Citgo station where he filled up with no lead
this morning. He wonders what people will think
when they find Lucille and him out here,
and then he remembers what he has to do.
He doesn't want to think anymore.
He says, "The hell with imagining.
Let them take care of the rest,"
and he puts the barrel to his throat
and pulls the trigger
hard, with his thumb.

# Building Desire and a House

You must imagine
you are going to have a lover,
everything about her,
inside and outside—
the color of her roof,
the distance between her windows,
her smooth foundation, like her instep or thighs,
the carpet fur you lie on,
the walls you belly up to,
each doorknob some bump or curve,
a shoulder or nose or nipple,
each door an opening,
and the fire in her stove
you can't wait to feed.

For now, though,
men stick around
to measure and cut holes,
to center studs, to sweat couplings,
to think about butt hinges and screw lengths.
You never thought
it would be so hard
to hook up a sewer line,
to jackhammer for five hours.
You just want to be inside her painted walls,
to shower and lie quietly on her rug.

Everything is a mess.
All you can do is wait
while nothing else waits—
not cleaning up wood, sawdust, and insulation scraps
each night,
not the fuchsias, roses, camellias,
or the maple and apple trees budding,
not the grass four inches higher
since the winter solstice,

not the drafting table
you impulsively offered
to build this week for your friend,
not the Mormons who come tonight
for their monthly visit,
not your daughter's Bat Mitzvah in two months,
not the warm front passing through,
not the sun, not the rain,

not the need for quiet
nor the desire for an end—

the hell with process, journey, and imagination,
everything proceeds,
you and nothing can wait.

# Colgate Shaving Cream

Inside this can
a blizzard waits for hot water.
A pillow of whipped cream,
well-behaved, wants to come out.
It wants to mingle with vanilla ice cream,
Non-yellowing white paint from Sears, tofu,
Wonder Bread, frosted light bulbs.

It wants to smell rice cooking,
taste angel food cake.
It wants to sit next to a bone china plate
and talk about the corners of a man's mouth.
It wants to make a life for itself,
like sperm spurting in my hand.

Instead, when it billows out
I catch stiff egg whites,
an empty cartoon balloon.

When I lather my face
it holds still like the frozen wave
of a Japanese woodcut,
makes a beard I cannot grow,
the hairless, smiling Buddha.
Santa. Father Time. Moses.

For a moment, it is the center of attention,
like the one ring lit up
at a three-ring circus. Then,
a razor comes by.
"Come," the blade commands the polar fur,
"Upper lip down, nose up.
There. Now, chin up."
It washes down the drain
like everyone leaving by one exit.

# *Three*

I would wake up suddenly
and ask my wife, What's that noise?
Did Wesley fall out of bed?
Nothing, she heard nothing.

Then I found pellets
lined up along the wall.
"Looks like rice, but if it's dark,
it's mice," my mother's voice
out of nowhere.

So I set three traps
and waited.

The first one got it in the neck,
but it was still alive. Black eyes
glowed while a flea
picked carefully through the gray fur.
The nude tail whipped. Occasionally
the body twitched.

The next trap disappeared
from the doorway of the furnace room.
Using a light, I found it
in a far corner, unreachable.
With red broccoli wire, I tied a magnet
to a long stick and pulled it out.
The trap dangled, one paw
flailed. The eyes again.

Both times
I took them into the garage
and held them in my left hand
while I rummaged through the tools.

Hammer or knife?
Splatter or gargle?
A piece of wood—walnut,
the size of my wallet,
was all I could hold easily,
use gently.

Later, the clarity, the stillness
of two gray mice,
brains oozing
through tightly shut eyes
in a Ziploc bag.

A third trap
disappeared from an attic doorway.
After that, we heard thumps, scratching,
rattles across the kitchen ceiling.

Three days, and I'd had enough.
I put on goggles, coveralls, a mask,
and got a ladder. I was afraid,
yet all I was doing was climbing up
to look for, to stop
a noise.
(How big? How much life left?)

This time, we were equals:
a small animal against
a man lightly protected
crawling in the cramped dim space
above his kitchen, both of us
on all fours. It
had a mouse trap attached, I
had a dim light.

Wires were everywhere. Yellow billows
of fiberglass insulation,
cobwebs, dust,

a constant draft, an offkey hum.
A toilet flushed, Boccherini lilted, duck roasted,
my knees ached.

What did you find? asked my wife.
Nothing, I said. I found nothing.

# A man should know his place

My father tells me
Confucius spoke of five relationships:
a ruler to his subjects,
a father to his son,
a brother to his brother,
a husband to his wife,
a friend to his friend.
Nothing about a man and a woman who are friends.

My best friend from high school, Oline,
is a tall, blond, green-eyed woman
who loves to talk, to watch television,
to eat spaghetti and *dim sum* with mayonnaise,
to buy gadgets like solar calculators
and both-sides-of-a-window washer.

In high school my parents did not allow me
to date white girls, so for years
Oline and I spent evenings
reading, talking, watching television,
and eating leftovers in her kitchen.
We're still best friends. We love to talk,
just talk. It's easy. It's serious.
My wife goes to sleep on the couch.

I thought I was unique
until my wife showed me a *New York Times* article
that said most men's best friends
are women who are not their wives.

Every few months something happens
to my friend Fred. For a few days
he yells at his kids, and nothing
that his wife Diana tries to do for him helps—

not food, not ignoring him or letting him alone
to dig in the strawberry bed.
One time when he was this way, I went there for dinner.
"What's wrong?" I asked.
"Questions," he said. "I've been asking big questions."
"Like what?" I asked.
"Important ones, that's all."
We ate dinner in silence.

Here are some questions:
How can a man be
friends with another man,
both telling secrets,
neither lying or taking too much?

At dinner in Toronto once,
a mathematician asked me what I did.
"I'm a househusband," I said.
"Then what soap operas do you watch?"

I wanted to tell him
about the ones in which his red wine,
roast beef, gravy, horseradish,
baked potato and sour cream get dumped
on his Harris tweed jacket and gray slacks
just before he remembers
there's no napkin in his lap.

Jean is my wife's friend, a mathematician.
I was in Gainesville and needed a place to stay.
She asked if I liked square dancing.
I swung her, bowed to her, promenaded her,
and held her hand on the dark path
from the lodge to the car.
That night in the guestroom bed
I had trouble sleeping.

There's another woman. Together we have cooked,
jogged, bicycled, gone to movies, built fences,
talked about our lovers, watched birds in the rain.

How can I not love
this woman that I love?
As a friend?

# Silences

1. My father sits across from me.
   He says nothing while he tries
   to write a certain Chinese word
   he has forgotten.

2. Two in the morning.
   I'm reading in the kitchen.
   The refrigerator fan turns off.

3. The door slams:
   our children leave for school.
   I put my hearing aid on.
   Chickadees and kinglets in the pine tree.

4. My wife and I lie in bed arguing.
   Long pauses.
   We're close but not touching.
   After we turn the lights out,
   I can hear her breathing.

5. Silence wedges its way in
   between sleep
   and morning's foggy sky.

6. I talk to a friend who moved to Portland.
   After I hang up the phone,
   a space in the air.

7. I turn off the table saw.
   Then I put chisels into their slots,
   hang up the hammers, sweep and pour
   sawdust into a bag,
   and turn off the lights.
   After closing the shop door, I pause.

8. Vaissade Road, on the Arcata Bottoms.
   The moon disappears above the fog.
   The slight hiss of a car
   on Samoa Road, to the south.
   To the east, orange lights in town.

9. I cast a fly onto Lake McCumber.
   Herons and geese fly in.
   They call a few times.
   The morning air holds its breath.

10. The ocean beach at night, between waves.

# Love, Habits, Heisenberg, Fruit

1.   by the tomatoes in the Co-op
   today I heard you say
   you love me

   the words were like Safeway specials
   avocados six for a dollar
   bananas fifteen cents a pound

   I didn't buy
   I didn't reach out

2.   we cannot
   at one time
   know both
   speed and position

   name the place
   I'll be there
   moving very fast

   figure out my speed
   you'll have trouble
   finding me

3.   from the kitchen
   I call your office and ask,
   "Where is she?"
   "I'm here," you call back,
   "but I'm in a hurry."

   You come home and ask,
   "What did you do here
   all day?"
   "Stay out of my way,"

I say. "Can't you see
I'm cooking dinner?"

4.  we have these habits
    I tell poems and friends
    what my secrets are

    you tell
    fellow mathematicians
    your secrets

    you go to my rare poetry readings
    I ask about your mathematician friends
    dressed up at parties
    we stay close to each other
    and listen

5.  "Nature puts up
    with our probings
    into its mysteries
    only on conditions.
    The more we clarify
    the secret of velocity
    the more deeply hidden
    becomes the secret of position."

    Werner Heisenberg
    was talking about electrons,
    but he knew about bodies
    and the uncertainty
    that comes with getting close.

6.  your lips find the curve of my neck
    my hands search the slope of your back

    you at the bend
    where I wait

I at the cleft
where you call

and want

such fruit
such fruit inside

# Trying to Fix These Last
## Two Weeks

Lying
in bed this morning,
the shade drawn,
the room all blue,
I am trying
to write you a letter or poem
that explains why
I don't love you.

Last night you and I were talking
about our best friends.
I wanted to say,
What do you do,
who do you tell,
when you feel this way?

Nothing unusual these two weeks:
I've cooked Chinese food
for a class,
driven our daughter Allison
to singing and piano lessons,
practiced violin with our son Wesley,
watched the lawn too long,
worked and worked on the leaky shower.

I should be able to fix this.
I should, I should.

Often when I am inside you,
you pull something
more than love and pain and life,
better than this emptiness,
out of me.

Yet all I can say then
is, I love you, I love you.

The camellia outside our window
has more pink and red flowers
than I have ever seen.
The fuchsia I thought I had killed
has green shoots
all over the trunk.

When this happened before,
was I less trapped and surrounded
by tools, cameras, junk mail,
school papers, poems,
wood chips, and laundry?

It's always the same,
always worse, waiting,
waiting for a cure.

Between us, married seventeen years,
behind us,
an Ashkenazi Jew,
a Canton Chinese,
you from New York,
I from California,
ten thousand years
of history, tradition, and family.
What a drag.

These two weeks
I've been trying
to match people up.
Nothing is going right.
Before he went to Arizona, Eric
didn't reach Lynn, who was afraid
to call him back. Joanne
liked Eric too, a complication. When she
heard about Andy, she was suspicious; he
sounded too good, too right.

All of these people, all
close to forty, all my friends.
And nothing has gone right.

Last week Lynn and I were alone
in her car on a long birdwatching trip.
The wind was picking up from the south,
the sky turning darker and darker.
Talking about her marriage and divorce,
she said, "You have to remember the good
times in the beginning, the sweetness,
to take you through the rough times."

My father-in-law is afraid to fix things.
Take enough time to tinker, I say,
and one of two things will happen:
you'll fix it or
you'll break it.
Right now something of mine is broken,
but I'm trying
to fix it.

# *Vivaldi's* La Primavera *Breaks Down*

I. Morning and Afternoon,
   *Allegro con molto rubato*

> Out back the maple tree conducts—
> branches howl up,
> leaves screech across,
> hang down and rustle, gust
> and hold still.
> In the shade, dark and green;
> near the top, brighter,
> wilder; then light, blue.
> Bend and straighten,
> again, again:
> morning, afternoon.
> Every year, these gusts—
> every day, he opens the window
> to let the air in.

II. Night or Early Morning,
   *Adagio expressivo*

> Through the frosty window,
> dark textures
> as lights flutter, larger, smaller—
> shadow and light; shadow, long rest.
> Late winter rises, recedes
> past New Year, then
> Chinese New Year, the spring
> festival of kites, Easter, equinox,
> Passover, Daylight Savings Time.
> The leaves outside wave slowly,
> he stands bare by the cooling stove,
> crawls back to bed. She's warm,
> she moans, she's asleep.

## III. All Day, Rondo
*Andante cantabile accelerando*

His love ebbs this time each year—
marriage bond, bondage, rhythm, beat—
he counts the time
in Vivaldi's A-minor Concerto with his son,
plays Copland's Bought a Cat and Wife
(honey, honey, she says) for the kids,
argues with his daughter, a new adult;
practices, draws curtains against the cold;
helps a friend move, says goodbye and waves,
a wild chorus of leaves;
waves and waves of doors closing,
lawn mowers mowing.

Love, the word. A dinner
with sweet and bitter herbs,
unleavened bread, rice, a roasted shank.
Wind that won't let up.

He cooks and loves like crows that swoop
and dip closer, closer to the ground,
while orioles chuckle and sass
from the pines, the birches,
the maple, always in the leaves.
Repeat. Repeat.

# Sequoia Park Zoo in the Spring

The peacock is on display
Behind the deep blue lagoon of his neck
his fanned tail and all his false golden eyes
look   sway   dip gently
with each careful step

As he turns slowly
it is the fluffed white down of the rump
and elegant brown tail      opened
like a perfect card hand
that turns to follow the speckled peahen
while the two real eyes and the other hundred
glazed and shimmering      look the other way

He folds it all
a curtain coming down on a chorus line
or a rummy player about to say Gin

Beneath the light blue sky   on trampled grass
a man and woman walk by
She wears a tank top   tight pants
his pale hand holds her
bare right shoulder   caresses her
long dark hair

Then the peacock calls
like a cat in heat
joy  hurt  desire  pleasure   all at once
he moans  I'm here   oww  oh
ah  everyone  come
here      now

# Summer, Shade, Knife, Nothing

For the window we installed this summer
we sewed a Roman shade—
six layers of quilted fabric
which made my wife's eyes water
each time we worked,
big enough to cover our queen-sized bed,
thirty feet of magnets to stick it tightly
against the windows,
a hundred feet of cord
looped through seventy rings
we sewed by hand through every layer,

the whole thing covering two double-hung
double-glazed windows mounted side by side,
trimmed with clear pine,
lacquered three times,
and rubbed smooth with fine steel wool.

My wife didn't want to start
the window or the shade.
Her parents were coming from Florida,
she had work to do at school, papers
to write, mathematical meetings to attend,
new juggling tricks to learn,
friends coming in from Portland and New Jersey.

I said, Do you want me to cook for them?
Of course, she said, if it's no trouble.
I'll get a second wok, I said,
and steamed large whole fish,
cooked the largest black mushrooms,
roasted Peking duck and rolled thin flour doilies,
all in the afternoons
after mornings measuring and sawing
two by fours, nailing sheetrock, painting.

We used to argue each time we danced
until we took lessons and I learned to lead.
But neither of us had ever built a shade,
so we argued each night.
Are you sure this is the right step?
Are we turning the right way?
We're not supposed to turn
the cloth this way now.
We'll have to do it over.

This morning I lay in bed
and looked at the shade,
look at the apple trees
through the new window,
at the clear pine plumb and level
to a sixteenth of an inch
over a length of five feet,
and the shade, square and tight.

I thought about the bargain
my wife and I have made—
she writes math papers,
makes the money I spend,
I make the evening meals, the home.

The shade's done. The guests are gone.
My wife is at her office.
It's quiet this morning.
Nothing's going on, yet
this nothing worries me,
this quiet time
I can't flavor with garlic, cut precisely,
or rearrange gracefully,
like this fog that has come and stayed
in the sky these last two weeks,
this fog I can do nothing about.

# October, The Arcata Bottoms

the land is smooth     flat
during the summers
there are barbed wire fences     cows
farmhouses     dark barns
high sky   fogged over   three months

today at dusk     after a blue hot day
hay bales squat
wood chip trucks square off
toward the sun on Samoa Boulevard

after ten years you expect
from these vague shapes
lines        humps        triangles
that wallow
in soft low fog now rising
not mist     not clouds
a cold night coming on

# Spring Cleaning

We have eight hens
and no rooster
yet the araucana,
who lays green eggs,
goes broody.
Every day for two weeks
when I pull her off the nest
to collect the eggs,
she flaps and squawks.
            *********

Between the chicken yard
and the overgrown quince
flowering red and full
of song sparrows and hummingbirds,
I find a dead rat
on bare, hard dirt.
The body is still warm and soft.
Why is it here in the sun?
I shoo a fly away.
            *********

Two years ago
the building inspector told us
to cut two vents
in our remodeled kitchen floor.
For air circulation, he said.
            *********

Last winter, I put poison
near the washing machine drain
because I'd found rat shit there
and under the washer and dryer.
            *********

Flies, green and shiny,
as big as Japanese beetles,
twenty or more a day in the house,
lolling and buzzing

on the kitchen window.
All the windows and doors have screens,
so I look under the sink for rotting garbage
and tap the walls and listen
for anything moving or scurrying.
Nothing, nothing.
         *********
Expecting to find maggots
crawling in stinking carcasses,
I pry up the vents
and shine a light all over.
Lots of rat shit and sawdust.
Still hoping, I take the light,
put on coveralls, boots, a skull cap,
and crawl under the house.
I've forgotten my gloves.
All I find is newspapers,
some rusty pipe from an old plumbing job,
some dusty dead leaves
and a few wires, disconnected.
         *********
I have other work to do—
a desk to build, songs to practice,
letters and poems to write,
chicken to cook,
dead fly stains to wash off the windows.
         *********

# What a Man and a Woman Desire and Want

He is inside her when he asks,
What's this lump on your breast?
Nothing, she says. It's nothing.
A few weeks later he asks again.
Her answer is the same.
He asks her to see the doctor.
Six weeks later he is impatient.
He says, I'll keep asking
until you see her.

The doctor says, Come back in two weeks.
It's your period,
not necessarily a good time.
Two weeks later, on a Monday,
the doctor sends her for a mammogram.
On Tuesday the surgeon says,
When would you like surgery,
Thursday or Monday?

At work, when he tells people,
they wish her well, and then
they go on typing, going to meetings, eating.

That night she tells him,
I'll go into surgery at seven-thirty.
There's no use getting up
that early. Just get the kids off to school.
I'll ride my bicycle to the hospital.

When they make love that night,
he turns the lights on.
He tries to see her
as the Amazon she wants to be,
without her right breast.

He remembers the night in Baltimore
when he photographed their month-old daughter
at her right breast
and a twenty-inch zucchini cradled
in her left arm. He wonders
who or what he will want,
who or what he will desire,
who or what he will love
tomorrow after her surgery.
He touches her breast gently,
but the lump pokes back firmly
like a deep rock in garden soil.
He kisses her, they kiss,
but it feels dangerous.

At ten the next day
he goes to the hospital.
He finds her asleep, grimacing.
She smells of ether and sweat,
and her right arm is taped to her belly.
He thinks he is calm, but later
he discovers he cannot remember
the three hours he sat there, wishing
for her to talk, to stop sleeping at midday,
to stop frowning, to get well and whole.

That evening he brings the kids,
but the six-year-old boy says
he just wants to go home,
there's nothing to do there
at the hospital.
The nine-year-old girl stares
at her mother, who tries
to be brave and talkative.
The boy keeps saying
he wants to go home.

When asked about the tumor,
the surgeon says it was small but malignant.
When she asks him about more surgery,

he says, I would take more, if it were my wife . . .
as if someone had taught him
about rapport with couples.
He looks at the surgeon,
a fat man who fills the doorway
and has trouble breathing. He thinks
about the surgeon in bed with his own wife,
and he wonders if the doctor would feel lumps
in her breast.

Wanting no more surgery,
she goes to another doctor, who says
If it were my wife, I'd cut it off.
Then you'd have no more cancer there.
Impeccable logic, they both agree.

She talks to a radiation therapist.
He says, If it were my wife—
but this woman wants no further pain,
no more uncertainty,
and all that these doctors can promise
is uncertainty, an x-ray question
every year. She is hooked to them
for life.

It is a question of want:
she does not want
to touch only one breast in the bath.
She does not want to admit
any sickness has been on her body.
She wants to remain an object of desire.
He wants her
to remain an object of desire.
He does not want any more
nights when he could not do enough
to help her lie without pain
or nights when she smelled sour and sharp
like a morgue or laboratory.
She does not want to find out
if stories of vomiting and lost hair

are true
and yet, he says to her in the station wagon
in the parking lot near her office,
he does not want to make a mistake
simply because of desire.
He does not want her whole
body filled with death
just because of desire.

They hold their breaths.
They hold hands.
They try to breathe.
They want to live,
to try to go on.

Fall.
Suddenly everything rushed down.
The Big Leaf Maple leaves grew old,
shrank, darkened from green to yellow to rust.
Clouds fogged and fattened. The sun
couldn't climb as high. A plague
of rain, all kinds. The hens
had fleas. Their feathers
were skeletons of plumes, their gray bars
and brown triangles turned as scrawny
as their feet, and sparrows ate
their feed, teased them
through the chicken wire. No eggs.

And light. Light moved back
into the ground.

Photo by Dar Spain

A native of Salt Lake City, Daryl Chinn is a poet-teacher-editor for the California Poets in the Schools program. He graduated from the University of California at Santa Barbara and has a master's degree from Johns Hopkins University. In addition to his teaching career, he has been a television cameraman, camera salesman, househusband, Chinese cooking teacher, father, carpenter, admissions counselor, and editor of a literary magazine. His poems have appeared in *The Florida Review, Pendulum, Center Stage, Toyon,* and *The Greenfield Review,* and he has edited four anthologies for California Poets in the Schools.